BRILLIANT BOATS

To Ann-Janine, Caroline and Suzanne – with thanks from Tony.
For Mister Mush and Scampy – A.P.

The Publisher thanks the National Maritime Museum, Greenwich for
their kind assistance in the development of this book.

 KINGFISHER

First published 2002 by Kingfisher
This edition published 2017 by Kingfisher
an imprint of Macmillan Children's Books
20 New Wharf Road, London N1 9RR

ISBN 978-0-7534-4460-3

Text copyright © 2002 by Tony Mitton
Illustrations © 2002 by Ant Parker
Cover design by Peter Clayman 2014

A CIP catalogue record for this book is
available from the British Library

Printed in China
9 8 7 6 5 4 3 2 1

BRILLIANT BOATS

Tony Mitton and Ant Parker

KINGFISHER

Boats are really brilliant for sailing us around. They travel through the water with a sloppy-slappy sound.

It's fun to go out boating, especially in the sun.
The water's cool and sparkly,
so come on everyone!

A boat sits on the water
like an empty bowl or cup.
It's hollow and it's full of air,
and that's what keeps it up.

An anchor holds you steady
when you're bobbing in a bay.
You wind a chain to raise it
when you want to sail away.

Over lakes and seas and rivers,
wind blows very strong.
Some boats have sails to catch it,
so it pushes them along.

To manage boats with masts and sails,
you need a clever crew.
The captain is the one in charge,
who tells them what to do.

A dinghy or a rowing boat is useful near the shore.

swish

swash

DORA

You make it travel backwards by pulling on each oar.

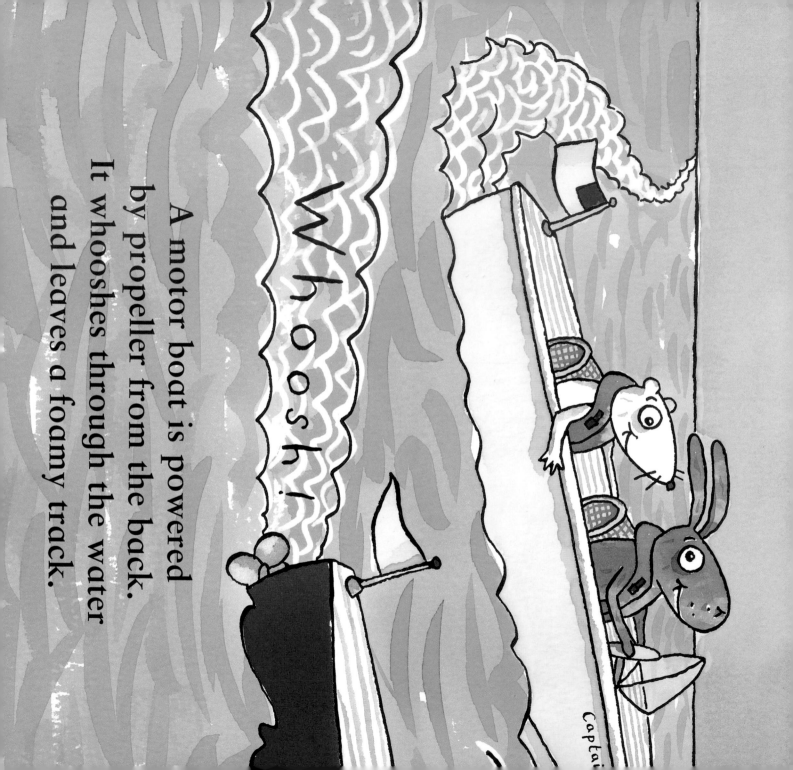

A motor boat is powered
by propeller from the back.
It whooshes through the water
and leaves a foamy track.

Whoosh!

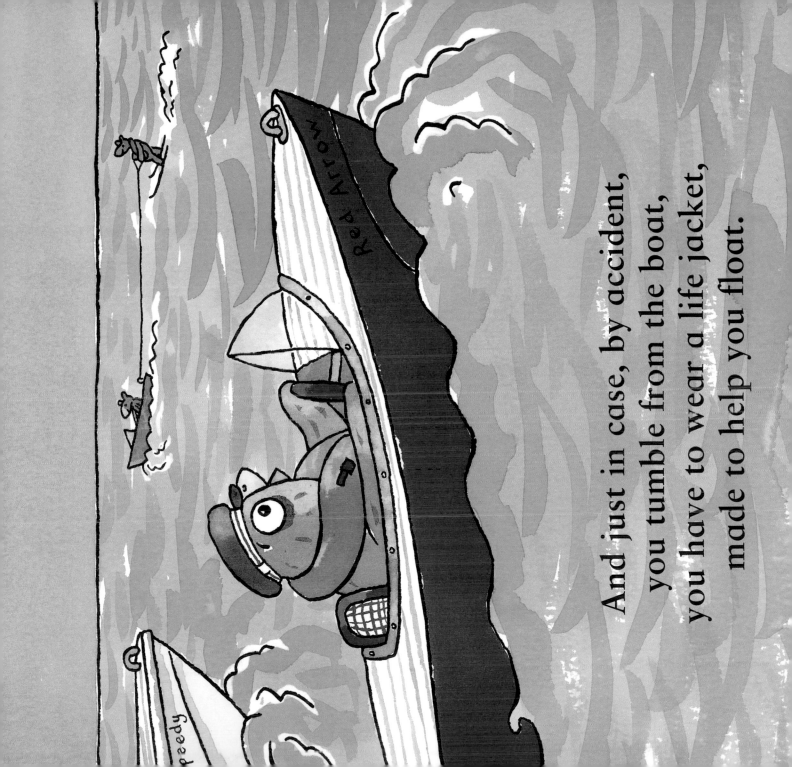

And just in case, by accident,
you tumble from the boat,
you have to wear a life jacket,
made to help you float.

Some boats go out fishing
where the ocean waves are steep.

Their nets are cast to catch the fish,
then haul them from the deep.

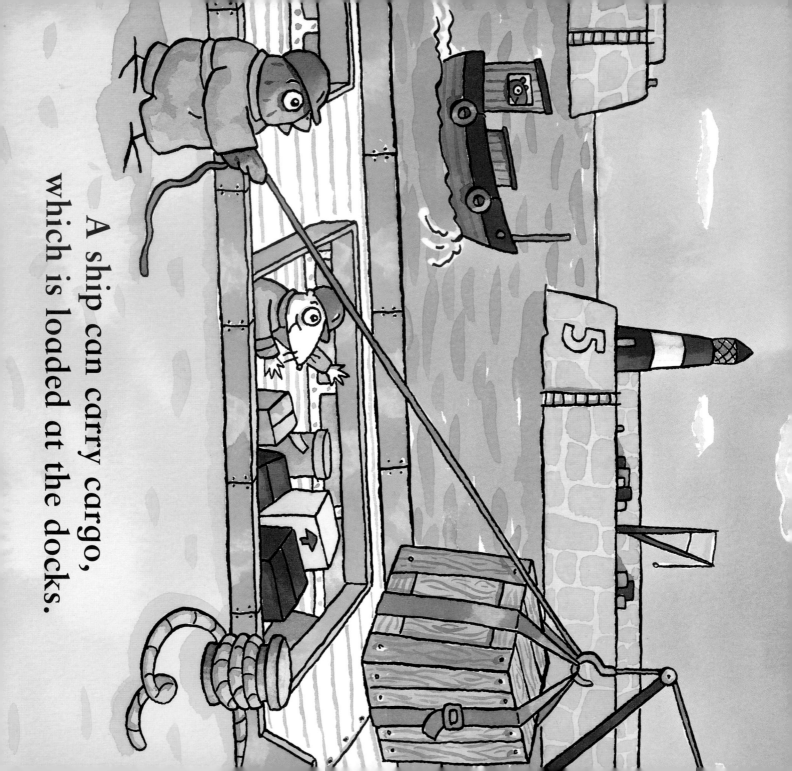

A ship can carry cargo, which is loaded at the docks.

Hup! Ho! Look out below!
Here comes a giant box.

A ferry carries cars and lorries where they need to go.

The people travel up above.
The vehicles stay below.

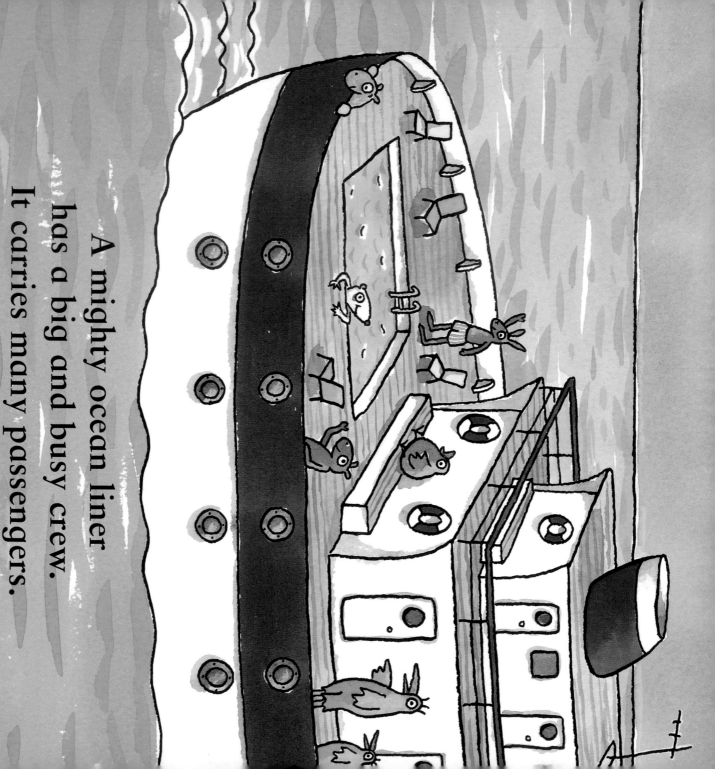

A mighty ocean liner
has a big and busy crew.
It carries many passengers.
They're waving now. Yoo-hoo!

The ship has cosy cabins
where the passengers can stay.
And out on deck they stroll about
and watch the sea, or play.

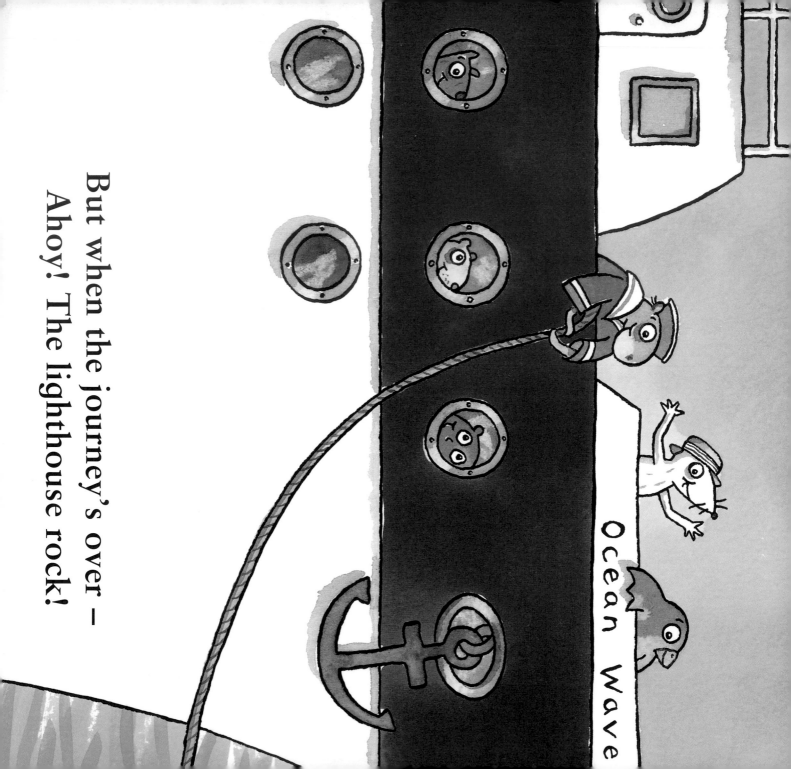

But when the journey's over –
Ahoy! The lighthouse rock!

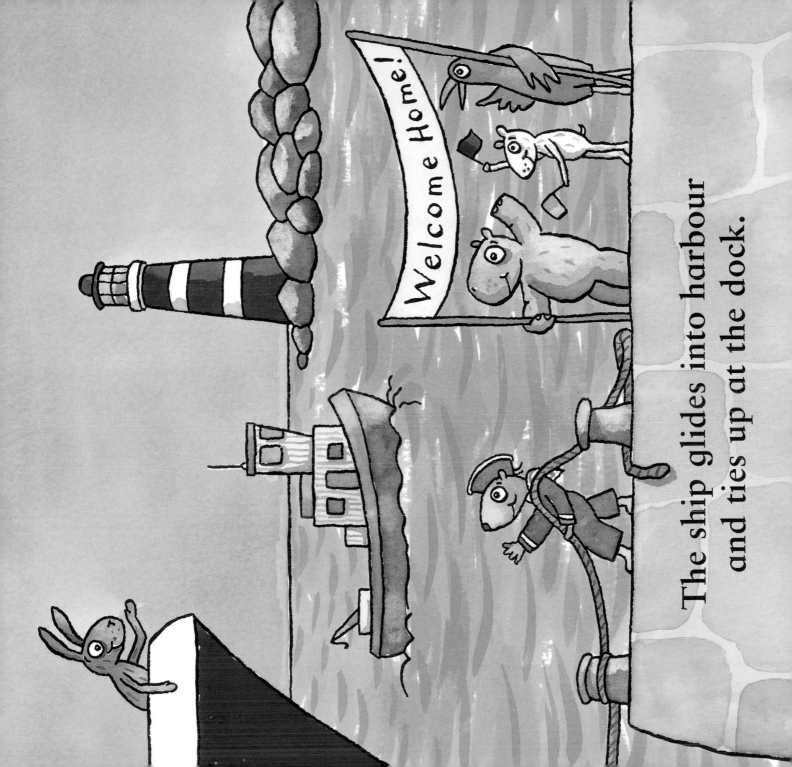

The ship glides into harbour
and ties up at the dock.

Boat bits

lighthouse

this is a tall building on the coast with a flashing light to guide ships and keep them away from rocks

propeller

this has **blades** which spin round very fast at the back of the boat and push against the water to move the boat forward

deck

this is the floor of a boat

MANDY

cabin

this is the little room where you sleep on board a boat

name

many boats are given names by their owners

anchor

this is a very heavy piece of metal with hooks which dig into the ground under the water to stop the boat drifting away

oars

these are long poles with flat **blades** at the end which push against the water to move the boat forward

cargo

this is the name for the goods that a ship transports

FRAGILE